G000090854

Anne & Mark

Photographs by Srdja Djukanovic

Text by Judith Campbell

Sidgwick & Jackson · LONDON

Half-title page: With Moriarty, Oak Grove stables, 1975

Title page: With Flame Gun (left) and Arthur of Troy
in the grounds of Oak Grove House, 1975

First published in Great Britain in 1976
Text copyright © 1976 by Judith Campbell
Photographs © 1976 by Srdja Djukanovic
Copyright © 1976 by Sidgwick and Jackson Limited

We are grateful to Mr and Mrs Peter Phillips
for so kindly allowing us to reproduce the pictures.
We are also grateful to George F. Barnes
for permission to reproduce the picture on p.7.
All photographs are copyright Srdja Djukanovic
with the exception of those on the above pages.

Designed by John Leath

ISBN 0 283 98330 2

Printed in Great Britain by
W. S. Cowell Ltd, Ipswich
for Sidgwick and Jackson Limited
1 Tavistock Chambers, Bloomsbury Way
London WC1A 2SG

CONTENTS

Childhood

Like everyone in the public eye Anne and Mark are subject to numerous people's often way-out conceptions of what they are really like, how they live and think, how they should earn and spend their money, what they should or should not occupy their time with. Reasonable, sometimes unreasonable, public interest is an acknowledged and inevitable part of being a member of the Royal Family, one that Princess Anne has always lived with and one that Mark Phillips has to accept because he fell in love with and married the Queen and Prince Philip's daughter. To the outsider one of the fascinations of this marriage between a princess and a young army officer is that while in some ways it is just like any other, in other ways it has to be extraordinary; while there are elements of complete normality about their life together, there are also elements quite outside the norm. But, in common with others, this marriage is founded on the characters of the two people concerned, and to a large extent individuals are moulded by background and upbringing.

The birth of a first child, Mark Anthony Peter, to Mr and Mrs Peter Phillips in 1948 was an absorbing event to themselves, and to their immediate relatives and friends. When Princess Anne was born in 1950 this was a most happy and engrossing event for her parents and all the Royal Family, but it was also a matter of public interest and pleasure. And although the previous over-sentimentalized vision of royal children had almost disappeared, after the Queen's accession and the move to Buckingham Palace there was still a section of the public which cherished an imaginary picture of the new sovereign's small daughter as a fictional, fairytale princess. Anne was a pretty child, but despite the fair curls and blue eyes, and for a time a nanny who put undue emphasis on her royal charges always being good, clean and tidy, she was an inappropriate candidate for such an unreal and sugary image. She was too young not to accept the less appealing nursery edicts as anything other than 'just life', but she refused, if unconsciously, to accept that in their nanny's eyes her brother Charles was somehow of more importance than herself. It was hard enough that he happened to be two years older.

The Queen and Prince Philip normally saw more of their children when young than many parents of the time whose households included a nursery ménage. During the weekends at Windsor and country holidays at Balmoral and Sandringham, they all shared the relaxed, happy relationship that the Royal Family enjoy together, with dogs and ponies to the fore, and plenty of picnics and rumbustious games. Except when the age gap made it a necessity, their parents made no

Mr and Mrs Peter Phillips holding Mark, aged eighteen months

Mrs Phillips with Mark, aged about three, and Mark's younger sister Sarah

material difference between the two elder children, but Anne still remembers her sense of outrage when Charles was taken to Westminster Abbey to see a short part of their mother's crowning ceremony while she was considered too young at three to do more than watch the processions from the Palace balcony.

All through her early childhood Anne had to prove to herself and others that she could do what Charles did, and more; she had to keep up. Brother and sister have always enjoyed each other's company; they share the same sense of the ridiculous which, as they grew up and began to attend some of the same public functions, proved to be a near fatal bond when catching each other's eye. To a different degree they have both inherited the Royal Family's talent for mimicry. Otherwise, by the time Anne left school almost the only interests she had in common with Charles were sailing, driving fast cars, and life in the open air. On most other matters they have always argued, usually amiably.

Being by nature brave and willing to try anything, always on the go and a bit of a tomboy gave Anne a veneer of being tough and completely self-contained. Where Charles, happy-natured but shy, was sensitive, amenable, thoughtful to others and very dependent on them, Anne was more of a loner, sometimes moody, and capable of throwing short-lived but tempestuous nursery scenes when thwarted. She was the originator of most of the youthful escapades, the first to shin up trees or lead occasional, and unpopular, sorties across the castle roofs at Windsor. When it came to riding Anne definitely had the edge on her brother. Charles

enjoyed the sport for a time, but he was not as talented and never as keen. His young sister's frequent and resounding exhortations to 'Use your LEGS, Charles!' had much to do with the fact that he gave up riding for some years, and was fifteen before the attractions of his father's chosen game of polo lured him back into the saddle.

In the years when Anne was establishing her prowess with ponies, indulging occasional day-dreams of living in times past as a simple country girl free as air, and continuing her education with Charles's governess, Mark Phillips was growing up on the family farm near Tewkesbury, in Gloucestershire. He was a good-looking boy, with an engaging grin and a ready laugh, though inclined to be shy. His life and interests centred on the countryside and the sports that go with it. When his father, a former major in the King's Dragoon Guards, sold the farm and went into business when Mark was about nine, the family moved to Great Somerford in Wiltshire, but their background of horses and hunting did not alter in any way.

Mark would have needed to be a complete changeling not to have imbibed the sporting atmosphere into which he was born. For him and his sister Sarah, horses were an established part of everyday existence, always there like dogs and furniture. Like Anne he was used to sitting on a small pony before he was three, and in age he just beat her to it when it came to being judged capable of riding off the leading rein. At

Mark, aged about ten, riding past the royal box at Badminton after winning the working pony class

7

Anne with the Queen Mother during the Trooping the Colour ceremony early in the sixties

six he was battling, usually with small success, with an over-strong and strong-willed pony of the same age. Two years later rider and pony had established a happy and often winning partnership, and Mark was showing above average ability.

In 1957 Prince Charles, aged nine, started at his father's old prep school, Cheam. In the same autumn Mark, two months his senior, set off for his first term as a boarder at Stouts Hill. He enjoyed the years there and is remembered as a good all-rounder, but especially good at games. He played rugger and soccer for the school, was in the first eleven at cricket, and showed a flair for athletics, with the long jump a speciality. In the holidays he returned to ponies and the Pony Club and the sport that seemed to come as naturally as walking.

By the time Anne was twelve the big decision had been taken to continue her education at boarding school. It was a totally new departure for a British princess, but the Queen and Prince Philip felt that preparation for life in the modern world needed to be considerably broader than anything more home education could provide, and Anne herself was keen to go. She was on good terms with her governess, although finding it increasingly irksome that there was someone who always had to know exactly where she was and what she was doing. Charles was away during term-time, returning for the holidays with stories of school friends and school life, and if it is only in retrospect

that Anne realizes how comparatively restricted her life was, she was certainly growing ever more restive and anxious to sample new ways and see new faces. So while Mark was in his second year at public school, Anne, who was just thirteen, was plunging into the noisy, communal life of Benenden School for Girls in Kent, an existence so utterly different to anything known before that it took a little while to adjust, especially to the ceaseless din. Once the first shock was over she seized the welcome opportunity of becoming just one in a crowd, and making friends with girls who were prepared to accept her as such. They found her happy and relaxed, interested in everything that went on, and fully capable of being as noisy and casual as anyone of her age.

It was not just a parental decision that sent Mark to Marlborough, one of the traditional public schools for those thinking of an army career. Much of his ancestry has a military flavour and his grandfather, Brigadier John Tiarks, was Colonel, King's Dragoon Guards, the regiment in which his father served during the Second World War. For as long as he could remember Mark had thought of the army as his chosen future, but his school examination results did not qualify him for direct entrance to Sandhurst.

Oddly enough Mark and Anne's school careers followed much of a pattern. Both were more athletically than academically minded, Mark continuing as a good all-rounder and, despite a back injury from rugger that eventually precluded both that game and any jumping, finishing up as captain of athletics. Anne was considered very intelligent with 'much more academic ability than she wanted to exercise', a variation on the theme 'could do better if he tried harder' that had cropped up in her father's school reports, but she infinitely preferred games and a weekly riding lesson to slogging away at some subject she did not care for. In the end she just had the edge on Mark by gaining one more 'O' level than he did, but they both have two 'A's.

By the time Anne left school in July 1968, when she was nearly eighteen, Mark had concluded his service in the ranks as a rifleman with the Royal Greenjackets, and having been accepted for officer training at Sandhurst the previous autumn was already embarked on his two-year course at the famous Military Academy, a time of achievement in his career, fun socially, and rapid acknowledgement of his horsemanship.

Anne was back home and feeling a little lost without the ordered school existence of the past five years, and without much opportunity for keeping up with ex-school friends who were all occupied with getting themselves jobs and flats, and the new independent life she could not make her own. The public engagements in her own right did not start until the following spring. In the meantime she had her own car, and social invitations that rolled in daily, but it took a little time to get to know acquaintances sufficiently well to be able to call them friends, and to readjust to restrictions scarcely noticed before being away from home.

Fortunately Anne has inherited the Queen and Prince Philip's philosophical talent for accepting life as it is, and instead of wasting time striving for the moon she set about seeing what could be fitted into the

limits of her life, horses and eventing playing an increasingly important role.

That year, 1968, was the year of the Olympics in Mexico, and at a post-Olympics party in the Whitbread cellar in the City Princess Anne was introduced to the awe-inspiring giants of her chosen sport, including the reserve rider, a good-looking but distinctly shy Officer Cadet Mark Phillips. They chatted politely, then parted to go their own ways for the next four years.

Courtship

At the beginning of those interim years there was speculation about Anne going to university. As her ex-headmistress affirmed, and contrary to some press opinions, the necessary qualifications were there. But even if the idea had appealed to her, like Prince Philip, Anne considers higher education is for those with the type of brain and future to benefit from it, not for those marking time while they try to decide what to do next.

A six-week course in French, cramming from 9 a.m. to 6.45 p.m. five days a week, cured Anne of any inclination for further crash forms of education, but produced sufficient command of the language for her to cope when necessary. Always there was the receding hope that a suitable, sufficiently absorbing job might turn up, but in the meantime Anne wanted to be really good at something and riding seemed the obvious answer. With the help and enthusiasm of her chosen trainer, Alison Oliver, wife of the well-known show-jumper, Alan Oliver, her determined effort to break into the tough world of adult eventing began to get under way.

The public side of Anne's life included travelling around Britain and much of the world. There were State visits with the Queen and Prince Philip to Australia, New Zealand, Austria, Canada, East Africa, the Far East and other countries, a brief visit to the U.S.A. with Prince Charles, another to Iran with Prince Philip. Wherever she goes Anne enjoys meeting people and seeing how they live, gathering impressions of what they think of the British way of life, and comparing geography learned at school with the actual facts. At one time she had an idea of contriving to get abroad unofficially and on her own, really getting to know a country and its people, as Charles was able to do in Australia, but it did not materialize. Increasingly she began to make visits in her own right, and the one to Ethiopia, although official, did include a three-day safari into the mountains on mules.

At first, apart from the travelling and the growing involvement with competitive riding, it was not easy to choose which way to go.

Mark Phillips was having no such problems. At that time his two great aims were to make a success of learning his trade as an efficient soldier and officer and to further his horsemanship to good effect. The two-year course at Sandhurst promised to fulfil both ambitions. He was proving able in his profession, and was well liked by his fellow cadets for his sense of humour, generosity and sportsmanship. Since he had long decided to devote his spare time to eventing, he picked that sport for the project which is required of each cadet during the long summer leave. Things were going well and life was good.

Anne was rapidly making her way into the eventing world too, slotting in what was becoming a more and more absorbing pastime with her increasing number of public engagements. There were twenty-five between the beginning of March and the end of October 1969, ranging from touring a car works – a good one for a mechanically minded girl who had had a fleeting desire to take an engineering course – launching a giant tanker, and attending an F.A. Cup Final, to flying out to a gas rig in the North Sea. A number of her engagements concerned young people, and putting to logical use the excellent rapport Anne has always enjoyed with her younger brothers and cousins and others of their age, she decided to become more involved with children. Becoming an active president of the Save the Children Fund was the first big step, becoming an equally live-wire Patron of the Riding for the Disabled Association, the second.

On that first round of public appearances Anne was astonished and touched by the size of the crowds and the warmth of their welcome. A great deal of press enthusiasm also attended her and Charles's slightly earlier emergence into the public eye, something that their father, tongue in cheek, attributed mostly to the public's discovery that the two young people were attractive and normally intelligent. Anne, feet as usual well on the ground, rated most of the press attention as novelty value.

In that year, between 2 April and 18 October, with the help, encouragement and know-how of Alison Oliver, Anne rode in twenty-one competitions, the majority being novice one-day horse trials. She experienced the usual luck and ill luck of all who ride horses, fell off a number of times, and showed an above average and heartening ability. But although the name of Mark Phillips was one impossible to miss in the eventing world, their ways were unlikely to cross at this stage unless he was schooling a young horse in some one-day trial. The Badminton entries for 1968, *the* three-day event of the year, included a horse called Rock On, owned and ridden by Officer Cadet Mark Phillips, who had started competing in horse trials only the previous year and had won or been placed wherever he entered.

One outcome of that first eventing season that was very important to Anne was that before it was ended she had been accepted by the eventing world as one of themselves, judged entirely on performance. If Anne could ride a horse she could ride a horse, it had nothing to do with who she was. This sport brought Anne great happiness, and the second season was more successful, a leap up the ladder towards the top rungs.

Mark left Sandhurst in July 1969 to be commissioned as a lieutenant in the Queen's Dragoon Guards,

leaving the Military Academy as one of his term's most promising cadets and runner-up for the coveted Sandhurst Sword of Honour, a presentation made to the best cadet. His regiment made it possible for the eventing to continue, and when, in the spring of 1971, Mark won the Open Intermediate class at the Rushall Horse Trials, Princess Anne was fourth. A few weeks later he triumphed at Badminton, and Anne, riding in only her second three-day event, finished fifth out of forty-eight starters. As competitors they were distinctly aware of each other, and Anne was discovering what she still knows, that the pundits are right in saying that when Mark Phillips is competing, more often than not he is the man to beat. A year later Mark was in the British team for the European Championships; Anne was riding as an individual. In the overall table he finished sixth, Anne first to become the new Individual European Champion. It was a long way to come in a short while.

Protocol and the eagle eye of the press never made it very easy for Princess Anne to get to know people well – meet a man more than once or twice and the headlines had a marriage pending. On first acquaintance she was anyway not very good at drawing out the reserved or the plain timid, although adept at dealing with the foolishly brash, and she was also sensitive about involving friends in the kind of publicity to which she was inured but they were not. It has never been easy to make Anne do anything she does not wish to, not that there was ever any suggestion of her marrying a man just because he was 'suitable'. She did not contemplate marriage for a long time to come. When she did marry it would be for love, and for his sake she hoped it would be someone who would find it easy to fit in with the conventions of royal life. She had found it much simpler to move in other people's circles than for them to cope with hers.

When Anne did fall in love it was with a man who through temperament, upbringing and career had much the same sense of self-discipline as herself, and if he knew little or nothing of royal restrictions Mark at least knew something about performing in the glare of publicity through competing internationally and from two experiences at the Olympics, as reserve in Mexico in 1968 and a team member at Munich in 1972.

As competitors and rivals Mark and Anne continued to meet up at intervals as part of the friendly easy-going world of event riders, but socially their paths crossed only occasionally. Then, after some horse trials in 1972, Mark and Princess Anne were invited to the same dinner-dance. Mark may be intrinsically a shy man but they were not exactly unacquainted, and for all his seemingly quiet personality he is noted for his sense of humour. Their mutual sport provided a good kicking off point, and an interesting and inexhaustible topic of conversation.

After Anne's Olympic hopes were shattered by the lameness of her horse, her motive in attending the Munich Games on foot that year could have been nothing more than natural interest in the fortunes of the British eventing team, but it is surmised that she and Mark contrived to see a great deal more of each other than the press were able to pinpoint. And in the circumstances, sufficiently fraught for him in any

Arriving at the theatre with Prince Philip and Prince Charles

case as an Olympic rider, it must have been doubly galling for Mark that his horse's cross-country performance was way below its own or its rider's true form.

Back home the friendship and mutual interest flourished, but in spite of all that has been said and implied, over Christmas 1972 and during the following January, February and March, there was no more to it than that. Mark considered himself a confirmed bachelor, and according to Anne frequently informed her of the fact. And it was hard on Anne that one of the most firmly believed myths about her was that her sole ambition after leaving school was to get married. It had never been true.

The nature of Anne and Mark's mutual sport made meeting easier, and if the eventing world suspected what was going on they wisely held their peace. Amongst the numerous candidates selected by the press as the man in Princess Anne's life, the debonair top event rider Richard Meade had long held a leading place, and good friend that he is to both of them he obligingly retained the image for some time. But the press were getting too attentive, and both Anne and Mark were well aware that with nothing definite between them, premature publicity about something that at the time did not exist could falsify a situation still nebulous to themselves. Dodging the press seemed the only thing to do.

At the time Mark was stationed at Catterick Camp in Yorkshire, and there were wonderful, stolen weekends when Anne stayed with his circumspect Commanding Officer; no doubt the entire regiment was aware of the fact but loyally keeping its mouth shut. But the rumours really began to fly after Anne was spotted more than once in the village of Great Somerford where the Phillips family live. They increased to fever point when it was known that Mark had spent two weekends at Sandringham, and then, when Anne drove him to Harwich en route to rejoin his regiment in Germany, their goodbye kiss was observed by a security guard.

Obviously the romance, engagement and marriage of the Queen's only daughter would be a matter of great public interest and intense press activity, but what did happen went way beyond acceptable bounds. Wherever they went Mark and Anne were hounded, followed, questioned, photographed. At one horse competition they were tracked by one hundred photographers, Italian, German and French as well as British. Three different Sunday papers reported them out together at three different places at the same time. The commotion affected their friends as well as themselves.

By March Mark and Anne, with the dedication typical of all top-class horsemen, were endeavouring to prepare two relatively inexperienced animals for Badminton. But even the Olivers' farm was besieged by reporters and cameramen, and the peace and seclusion necessary for such schooling became almost impossible. It may be difficult for the uninitiated to realize the extreme sensitivity of high-bred horses,

Mr and Mrs Phillips (left) *at a U.S. Equestrian Society party in Massachusetts, summer 1975*

trained to the minute for an arduous competition and only too easily distracted and upset, but, other considerations apart, the single-minded application that all world-class sportsmen bring to their sport, whatever it may be, is well known. Small wonder some members of the press received the rough edge of Princess Anne's tongue.

No doubt the official denials of an engagement added fuel to the fire, but even then, absurd as it seemed to the outside world, the comment 'Only friendship and a mutual interest' was still basically true. There was no engagement, secret or by implication, and since they share a streak of obstinacy, maybe the imminent engagement and marriage quoted almost daily by the papers determined Anne and Mark not to discuss either contingency with each other. The situation, with the lack of privacy and the immediate exigencies of Badminton, gave little opportunity for discussing what is perhaps the most important decision in life.

Then, in mid-April, the tensions of Badminton behind them, they knew; the most natural thing in the world was to become engaged. But no wonder that when Mark asked Anne to marry him and she accepted they decided to keep their happy and very personal secret to themselves for a while.

The public announcement was made on 29 May 1973 at Balmoral Castle, where all the immediate family were spending the Spring Bank Holiday weekend. Then all the world knew officially the happy news it had been waiting for and had long surmised; the Queen and Prince Philip announced with the greatest pleasure 'the betrothal of their beloved daughter The Princess Anne to Lieutenant Mark Phillips'.

The matters of protocol bound up with all royal weddings were set in motion, the arrangements got under way, recognition and good wishes from people all over the world poured in, with a flood of much appreciated wedding presents to follow. In the normal order of army promotion Mark became a captain.

There was some inevitable carping, and some of it hurt because it was misinformed. After all, the cost of the wedding was nothing to do with the bridal pair, and since, though enhanced by many of the splendid trappings of a State occasion, it was a family wedding, the Queen and Prince Philip bore the brunt of the cost. There was criticism about using *Britannia* as a base for the Caribbean honeymoon, but to be ready for the Queen and Prince Philip's forthcoming visit to New Zealand the royal yacht had anyway to sail via the West Indies. There were adverse comments about not utilizing a non-existent 'empty house' in Windsor Great Park as a home, and about the special 'privilege' of a house provided by the army, though it is normal procedure for all married officers posted as instructors to Sandhurst to have quarters allocated to them.

Thought was given to having the wedding in St George's Chapel at Windsor Castle, but eventually it was decided they should make their marriage vows in Westminster Abbey, the church where the Queen and Prince Philip had made theirs twenty-six years before almost to the day.

And so, on Wednesday 14 November 1973, the crowds were out waiting patiently in the chilly autumn air, with troops lining the route leading from Buckingham Palace to the Abbey. Soon the cheers mingled with the clatter of hooves as the horse-drawn carriages with attendant Household Cavalry escorts went by, a part of the splendid pageantry that is British tradition and equalled by no other country. The Scottish State Coach carrying the Queen, the Queen Mother, the Prince of Wales and Prince Andrew headed the procession. At the end came the Glass Coach carrying the bride, Her Royal Highness the Princess Anne, Fourth in Succession, Second Lady in the Land, lovely, composed, and very happy, escorted by her father, His Royal Highness the Duke of Edinburgh.

Within the realms of possibility Mark and Anne wanted their wedding to be a simple one. Inside the Abbey there was colour and beauty, flowers, glorious music and singing, the bridegroom and best man resplendent in full-dress uniform, a fanfare of trumpets to greet the bride, the Honourable Corps of Gentlemen at Arms on duty in the lanterns and choir, the Yeomen of the Guard in the nave. The Archbishop of Canterbury conducted the service, assisted by the Dean of Westminster; the guests numbered around 1,500 and included foreign royalty, distinguished statesmen, and representatives from all over the Commonwealth. There were an estimated 5,000,000 people watching on television. Nevertheless, the form of service was essentially the same as that used at every church wedding in the land, the bride was attended by only her nine-year-old cousin, Sarah Armstrong-Jones, and her youngest brother Edward. No intrusive television camera attempted to mirror the Queen's reactions in her position as mother of the bride, no camera intruded when bride and groom made their solemn vows. Within the realms of possibility the wedding was, as Anne and Mark wished, a family affair.

Army Life and Public Life

It is not exactly usual for an army officer's wife to have acquired previous military experience through holding high honorary rank with three distinguished regiments, or to have first-hand acquaintance with the same mark of tank as that equipping her husband's regiment. But Princess Anne became Colonel-in-Chief of the 14/20th Hussars when she was eighteen, and had the fun and challenge of driving one of their Chieftain tanks when visiting them in Germany. Later she also accepted the same appointment with the Worcestershire and Sherwood Foresters, and with the 8th Canadian Hussars.

In June 1972, six months before her marriage, Princess Anne took the Sovereign's Parade and presented the Sword of Honour at the Royal Military Academy, Sandhurst. The following March Mark began his duties there as an instructor attached to New College, and they moved into Oak Grove House, where Anne began her life as an army captain's wife.

Nowadays all British army officers have to go through Sandhurst. There are various methods of entry and three main courses, but to qualify all cadets have to reach the same high standard of 'officer quality and military skills'. The company officers who provide general military instruction come from every regiment and corps in the British army, and are very carefully selected for what is a most responsible job.

New College looks after cadets taking the Standard Military Course, which basically concerns infantry tactics. By September 1973 Mark had his own platoon and was responsible for taking the twenty-five to thirty men right through the then twenty-five-week course. The administration alone keeps a platoon commander fully occupied, but the personnel side is also a large part of the job. Each day lasts as long as is necessary to get through the scheduled and unscheduled work and that often means an early morning start and working late into the night.

During the course Mark organized and went on the frequent 'small' exercises, and helped run the four major ones, when he accompanied his men to Dartmoor, Wales and East Anglia, winding up with two weeks in Malta.

From March 1974 until he finished at Sandhurst in September 1976 he was employed as Company Second-in-Command on the slightly differently organized Regular Career Course, and then took over Inkerman Company in the same capacity. For four months out of the twelve this entailed dealing with two strata of cadets, the seniors nearing the end of their military phase, with whom he spent a lot of time out on exercises, and the new intake just starting the course. This necessitated interviewing each new cadet in depth during the first couple of months to discover his future aspirations in the Service, to explain exactly the requirements of his choice, and finally to assess each man's qualifications and suitability in a detailed written report. All this type of work has to be fitted in out of normal working hours.

As well as routine administration Mark and his Company Commander were responsible for anything ranging from looking after the interests of the occasional law-breaker – irregularities commonly concerning drink or speeding – to checking the arrangements for a Company discothèque and supervising early morning sports and weekend activities.

It was a full and interesting life, but it is easy to understand why Mark has commented that one of his and Anne's problems is not getting enough time together. In his second instructional job, however, two things made life easier. He was giving fewer lectures, a facet of instructing with which he had wrestled and got by, but which never came easily to someone who, until 'warmed up' and relaxed, can find it difficult to express himself and put his thoughts across clearly. And within limits it was then also possible sometimes to rearrange his programme so that schooling his horses could be fitted in during the morning, and the military time and work made up in the evening.

The army is keen on the good image provided by sport, and its international and Olympic athletes are encouraged and often given every facility. As a troop leader in his regiment before his marriage Mark could be more easily spared from his duties than he could as a Sandhurst instructor, and now that he is married to Princess Anne he has to be particularly meticulous in doing a full day's military work on top of the tough top-level equestrian training.

In early 1976, like any other potential Olympic athlete, Anne too had to concentrate on training. Ever since she reached the top it has been her declared ambition to ride for her country in the Olympics, but although like Mark she was picked for the selector's short list on the long and short term record of herself and her horse, she knew that the final team of four riders and a reserve would not be chosen until shortly before leaving for Canada. The team is finally selected entirely on merit, and one of the first requisites is that both horse and rider should be at a peak of training and fitness.

For this Olympic build-up, and before and during the normal eventing season, whenever possible and however early the hour, Mark and Anne school their horses together, and when Mark's duties prevent him, his wife, with Alison Oliver's help, copes with his animals as well as her own. However absorbing, it is a strenuous and time-consuming occupation, and during the crucial weeks of early 1976 the Princess did not take on quite her usual number of public engagements. But although, like her father, Anne does not regard the ability to fulfil public engagements well as a particularly gainful achievement – unlike representing one's country internationally or at the Olympics – she does accept King George V's view of the Royal Family as a 'firm', and her public engagements are her contribution.

When Princess Anne began her public life she shared one of the Queen's ladies-in-waiting, a friend

On Columbus before the dressage at Badminton, spring 1973

to accompany her whether out shopping or at a function in her own right, to help her decide which of these engagements to accept, and to deal with the increasing flow of correspondence. Before long, however, Anne, like Charles, had her own office and staff at Buckingham Palace and was fully embarked on the family's curiously independent working life, in which, close as they are in most matters, they are often quite unaware of each other's public commitments.

Nowadays the bulk of Anne's public life is still organized from her office in the Palace, which is run by her two secretaries and to which she drives herself several times a week. The flow of letters now often resembles a flood. There are the personal ones requiring a personal answer, and then all the others, official, requesting, begging, amusing, sometimes cranky, occasionally critical, all to be read and pondered over before being handed over with instructions to the staff. The invitations to public engagements, sufficient to fill up every day for the coming year, have to be sifted, considered in order of importance, suitability and personal interest, and then whittled down to a manageable number. Once an invitation is accepted the ball really gets rolling. There are such matters as informing the Lord Lieutenant concerned, checking travelling arrangements, determining the exact distances between A and B, and liaising with the appropriate authorities for scheduling the whole affair for split-second timing. If the engagement concerns another

country, a further complication is trying to work out the likely weather conditions there six months ahead so that suitable clothes can be planned.

Much of this side of it is the province of the two ladies-in-waiting, one full, one part time, who with the secretaries look after the official side of the Princess's life. Their salaries and all the other expenses connected with her royal commitments are paid for out of the annuity provided for Princess Anne from the Civil List; this was increased to £35,000 on her marriage.

Anne writes her own speeches, delivers them in the same informal idiom in which she talks, and believes in brevity. She does not aspire to the wit of her father and elder brother, both exceptional speakers, but is usually pungent, amusing and to the point. The Queen and Prince Philip are always diligent about their 'homework', and Anne has been brought up in the same tradition so that her comments on whatever she is being shown are well-informed and interested. As a child, making conversation could be a nightmare and there were some awful meals with guests at Balmoral when Anne sat in stony silence, but as she grew older she set out to conquer the difficulty, and did.

Anne sometimes disregards the royal requirement to tread warily; she does not suffer fools gladly and can be impatient with someone who is only trying to be polite and say the right thing. Her sharp line in repartee can make her appear unintentionally brusque, and at functions with her family in the early days she did not always shine, tending to remain in the background and reserve her smile for her 'turn'. She was sometimes accused of looking bored, which as a 'doer' rather than a 'watcher' she may well have been, though she was more probably tired. But the vast majority of the thousands of people she meets of all ages, social classes and races are captivated by Anne's down-to-earth outlook, her genuine liking for people – other than the fawners – her sense of humour, and her underlying kindness, and because, like the Queen, she is transparently incapable of pretending to be anything she is not.

The only times that Mark's Palace duties take precedence over his military ones are when, in his capacity as A.D.C. to the Queen, he is required for a State visit, but he can sometimes accompany Anne to an evening function. During official leave in 1975, Mark and Anne had the fun of going to the Ledyard Horse Trials in America as members of the British eventing team. During an earlier leave they paid an official visit to Australia.

All royal visits are marathons of timing and endurance, trying to fit into a few days as many functions as possible to cover the widest possible field of interests. Presentations, official receptions, luncheons and dinners are part of the accepted pattern, but the Australians also based much of the programme on their guests' known interest in children and horses. They were able to see the Australian side of the Save the Children Fund, the Riding for the Disabled Association, and the St John's Ambulance Brigade, as well as many other organizations and projects.

It was all interesting and worthwhile, mostly

pleasurable, and a big success. Between 23 April and 6 May it involved about seventy-seven ceremonies of one kind and another, and, not counting the flight out and back, included seventeen hours of flying time in Australia covering nearly 10,000 kilometres, touching down, sometimes twice or more, at Sydney, Canberra, Adelaide, Port Lincoln, Alice Springs, Tennant Creek, Katherine, Darwin, Paraburdoo, Karratha, Geraldton and Perth. They travelled a further 800 kilometres by car. The distances walked are unrecorded and so too are the hours of standing. Anne and Mark are young and physically fit from their sport, which is as well because this sort of work demands stamina. It can mean carrying on regardless of having developed flu or any other complaint, and always means headaches, backache and aching feet at some stage, and a dependence on a kind of official 'patter', which Mark has still to acquire, to help carry you through. Back home it takes time, sometimes weeks, to readjust.

Before marriage 'security' was a word Mark only thought of in its military context. But he soon grew used to the presence of Anne's detective, one of the admirable, unobtrusive men who have been part of her life for as long as she can remember. Mark also subscribes wholeheartedly to the Royal Family's outlook on the subject – fall in with any precautions the police consider necessary, then get on with the business in hand. Even in this violent age the only possible attitude on the part of the Royal Family is to assume that the despicable threats to them that crop up from time to time are hoaxes. But the terrifying and bizarre incident that took place on the evening of 20 March 1974 when a gunman tried to kidnap the Princess was far from being an unimplemented joke.

Anne and Mark were being driven, with Rowena Brassey, the Princess's lady-in-waiting, and Inspector Beaton, her personal police officer, back to the Palace after an official engagement, when a white car swerved in front of them and forced their chauffeur to stop in the Mall. The driver approached, and as the Inspector got out to see what was wrong the man shot and wounded him in the shoulder. The Inspector fired back but missed, and when his gun then jammed a threat to shoot the Princess forced him to put it down. In the meantime the gunman was trying to open the car door that Mark and Anne were strug-

gling to keep shut, and demanding that the Princess went with him.

In the ensuing minutes of confusion, great danger and exceptional courage, Inspector Beaton was shot in the hand he used to screen the back window, and then in the stomach while trying to shield the Princess with his own body. Mr Callender, the chauffeur, was shot in the chest while bravely clinging to the assailant's arm, and Mr McConnell, a passing journalist who ran to help, was also wounded in the chest. The first police officer on the scene was badly wounded in the stomach, a man called Mr Martin, who came to his assistance, drove his car in front of the abductor's to prevent a get-away, and Mr Russell, another passer-by, punched the man on the back of the head, was fired at and missed, and then punched him again in the face as he once more attempted to drag the Princess from the car. The gunman eventually tried to run away but was overpowered by an unarmed policeman who knocked him down.

For Anne and Mark it was a kind of ghastly, unbelievable tug-of-war, with Mark gripping his wife round the waist and trying to pull her back as the man repeatedly seized her by the arm and threatened to shoot her if she did not go with him. Anger, and distress about the brave men wounded in their defence, were their uppermost feelings at the time, and while still being pulled and threatened Anne, ignoring the gun and refusing point blank to go with her assailant, with great coolness and presence of mind tried to distract him by engaging him in conversation.

It was a shocking incident, made more so by its utter improbability. All those who showed such gallantry and total disregard for their own safety were rewarded, with Inspector James Beaton heading the list; he received the George Cross, the civil equivalent of the Victoria Cross. And if in the future Anne and Mark find it hard to believe that such a thing really happened, they have the awards in the Victorian Order which are made personally by the Queen. The Princess was appointed a Dame Grand Cross (G.C.V.O.), to show the Queen's 'appreciation and to express her admiration of the Princess's calm and brave behaviour . . .' And to '. . . recognise the excellent conduct of Captain Mark Phillips . . .', the Queen appointed him a Commander (C.V.O.), both awards to be dated 15 August 1974.

Eventing - A Shared Sport

Like Mark, Anne started riding mainly because horses and ponies were there, but whereas he continued simply because he liked it better than anything else and was good at it, Anne's motives were more complex.

Riding provided enjoyable speed and a spice of adventure, it was fun, and it was a good method of avoiding governess supervision for a while. It was also the means of 'doing her own thing'. As she got older riding became a way of proving that success need not

be related to position in life – that same emphasis on 'the man, not the Prince' that has always been her father's incentive, and motivates Charles's private challenges. A horse is no respecter of rank – either you can ride it well, or you cannot.

To prove her point Anne chose eventing, or combined training from the French Concours Complet d'Equitation, a tough sport, more genuinely amateur than most, and at that time not very well known. By 1976 at least one journalist was still alluding to Anne and Mark's mutual interest as show-jumping.

Mark does occasionally show-jump, but that is a very different sport to the one they have made their own, to become the only Olympic-standard husband and wife team in the world. Eventing tests the all-round horseman and horse: the dressage phase is designed to demonstrate the animal's obedience, suppleness and impulsion; it is followed by a trial of their combined stamina and speed across country and over fixed obstacles, and lastly by a trial of their sustained fitness and control through a small course of show fences.

One-day horse trials are devised for those without the means or ambition to go higher. These trials are also used by three-day eventers to school novice horses, and by aspiring competitors trying to qualify for the supreme test, the three-day events that, for some, are the doorway to international and Olympic competing.

All events start with a dressage test. The three-day version has an extended speed and endurance phase with roads and tracks, a steeplechase and an arduous cross-country, in all about fourteen miles, with a tight time limit; the show-jumping takes place on the third day. There are stringent veterinary tests for the horses throughout. In 1976 when Mark rode two horses all round Badminton and another part of the way he covered forty-six miles in one day, taking 122 fences at speed and receiving an involuntary ducking in the lake.

On Goodwill, Hickstead, summer 1973

Mark was already way up top when Anne was just beginning. When she went to Alison Oliver her assets were good balance and natural rhythm, plenty of nerve, and the fact that horses go well for her. It was a blessing for Alison that her pupil had the ability to grasp quickly what was required and then act on that knowledge, and, later, to take over a horse's training and continue from that point on her own. Anne's experience of competitive riding was limited to Pony Club standard, her experience of adult eventing, nil. She had no technical knowledge, and was without the essential basis of having schooled and trained horses. Her own animals were as inexperienced as herself, the famous Doublet, bred by the Queen as a potential polo pony, being then a complete novice with which Anne did not see eye to eye.

With Alison's irreplaceable help, a lot of concentrated training when time allowed, much fun, falls, disappointments, successes, luck both good and ill, Anne arrived at the top, like Mark in an impressively short time.

Acknowledged as one of the world's top event riders, Anne no longer needed to prove herself to herself or anyone else, only to stay up top, and achieve the ultimate ambition – to ride for Britain in the Olympics. Now she has the added fun and incentive of trying to keep level in competition with Mark, and for both the sport has taken on new dimensions of mutual enjoyment.

Sandhurst is a good place for horsemen. Until 1939 riding was part of the curriculum. Now a thriving riding club provides facilities, including an indoor

school, an outside jumping arena, a space for dressage, and the Barossa military training area, at times available to the Sandhurst riders, and the site of the cross-country designed and built by Mark and Anne for the 1976 Army Horse Trials.

Any cadet or staff member can keep a horse, at his own expense, in the extensive stabling at Sandhurst. Having her own contingent close by the house was a new joy for Anne, for the first time able to incorporate her horses into everyday life. Anne and Mark do all their own training on the flat, and the cantering and jumping, leaving the exercising to the girl grooms because two people cannot cope entirely with the six horses that make up Anne and Mark's usual combined string during the season. Riding each other's animals is very helpful during the months of hard work and schooling which go into preparing for a three-day event. Mark, a forceful rider, uses his strength and weight to sort out one of Anne's horses if it is being particularly uncooperative, and Anne's more calming approach is excellent if one of Mark's is feeling extra sensitive.

They have both had their share of disasters. Mark's Rock On, a very good horse, died under an anaesthetic. After winning the European Championship, Doublet's subsequent lameness put paid to any hopes Anne had of the 1972 Olympics; she also had to defend her title at Kiev with the then comparatively inexperienced Goodwill, and they crashed at the second fence. Mark was within an ace of winning the 1974 Individual World Championship with the brilliant and potential Olympic hope, Columbus, when the horse slipped the ligament off its hock and is still recovering. That same year Anne retired from Badminton when Doublet hit a steeplechase fence. A few weeks later when riding quietly at Windsor the horse's hind leg snapped, possibly because of an unsuspected hair-line fracture. And, as with all true horsemen, for Mark and Anne these tragedies do not just concern valuable competitive animals, for their horses are the dear companions of their everyday lives.

Now Anne and Mark have each other to help out when things go wrong, and to share the excitement when they go right. Mutual rapport may sometimes be lacking when, taking turn about to drive the horse-box home after an event, one may be treading on air after winning, the other down in the dumps after a poor day. But when Anne's Olympic training was interrupted at a crucial moment in the spring of 1976 by a bad fall with a young horse, she had Mark to help her get going again and to boost her morale. And Anne could console Mark when, at the final Olympic work-out before naming the team, her Goodwill put up an excellent performance but the brilliant, temperamental Favour, his number one horse, was disappointing.

These two have the right attitude towards competing. They spare nothing in preparing their horses and themselves for the competition that is the target, and then, although always aware of their horse as a sentient partner, they go all out to win. But for both eventing is first and foremost a sport, and if the stresses of galloping over big fences make the cross-country phase only consciously enjoyable in retro-

Ledyard Farm, Massachusetts, summer 1975

spect, enjoyment is still the criterion, and they will never allow their sport to become so deadly serious that it ceases altogether to be fun.

All top-ranking event riders make international and Olympic competing their ultimate ambition, but even at those pinnacles Anne and Mark consider that the prestige which is implicit in being asked to ride for one's country is at least as important as winning medals.

After the final work-out at Osberton on 30 June, Anne and Goodwill seemed certain of their team place, barring accidents, but Mark's position was less sure. As a rider he had all the ability and the advantage of previous Olympic experience, and he had won the Badminton Horse Trials three times, but although he won the Osberton trial with his second string, the talented Persian Holiday, the horse had not done a great deal since being off work with leg trouble in 1975. It was a toss-up between Mark Phillips and Hugh Thomas. Six riders and seven horses went for final training at Ascot, and the team was selected on 7 July. It consisted of Princess Anne, European Champion in 1971, runner-up in 1975, the first member of the Royal Family to compete in the Olympics, with her excellent partner Goodwill; Lucinda Prior-Palmer, reigning European Champion and winner of Badminton 1973, with Be Fair; the triple Olympic gold medallist Richard Meade with Jacob Jones; and Hugh Thomas with Playamar, third in the 1974 World Championships. As in the 1968 Olympics in Mexico,

Mark was reserve, free to take either Favour or Persian Holiday. Though it must have been a great disappointment for one who only a few months previously appeared to have the pick of four good horses and is without doubt one of the best riders, at least he was there.

If the modicum of necessary luck was not with Britain in the 1976 Olympics, so that in spite of Be Fair and Playamar's heartening efforts their subsequent unsoundness eliminated the team, from a personal viewpoint Princess Anne achieved much of her ambition. Tension and unfortunate applause spoiled Goodwill's dressage calm, and a boggy take-off at fence nineteen resulted in a very nasty fall, badly winding them both, but they completed the competition in twenty-fourth place.

A visit to the Mall Galleries in October 1975 when Princess Anne opened the exhibition of the Royal Institute of Oil Painters

Country Life

When Mark finished at Sandhurst in September 1976 he and Anne stayed on at Oak Grove, Mark returning there at weekends from the three-month Junior Command and Staff Course at Warminster, by chance not far from his and Anne's new home, Gatcombe Park, in Gloucestershire.

For country lovers with interests to do with horses and the necessity of living within reasonable distance of London and the Buckingham Palace office, Gatcombe Park could scarcely be bettered. The lovely, stone-built eighteenth-century house is certainly not palatial, but it is much larger than the Sandhurst house. Some extra domestic help is likely to be needed to supplement the Oak Grove staff of butler/valet, cook/housekeeper, a daily, and the Princess's lady's-maid – indispensable because royal duties demand immaculate clothes – but Anne and Mark are unlikely to change their style of home life to any great degree.

At Sandhurst, chiefly because of lack of time, their social life was not very extensive. Mark attended the instructors' social activities for men only, and when Anne was free she went along to the infrequent ladies' nights. Occasionally they gave or went to the kind of informal party instructors organize in their various quarters. Several times they managed to escape public

At the Badminton Horse Trials, 1976

notice sitting in the stands with the rest of the staff to watch the Sovereign's Parade. They enjoyed the occasional good film, usually contriving to remain unrecognized, but otherwise were thankful for a quiet evening at home.

No doubt Anne and Mark will enjoy sometimes sharing the beauties of their new home with relatives and friends, but most of their socializing is likely to have a farming or equestrian background. With the help of the existing farm staff of three and a forester, they will continue to run the 200 acres of woodland, the 530 acres of wheat and barley and the 100 head of beef breeding cattle as a viable farming enterprise. For horses the estate promises to be a paradise.

The actual competing side of Anne and Mark's life with horses is very important to them, but it is not everything. When the season ends there are young animals to work, hunting, the sheer pleasure of just riding. But as all horse owners appreciate, unlike bicycles, after use the creatures cannot just be parked and left. Whenever time allows, Anne and Mark are at the stables, trundling wheelbarrows, toting buckets, bandaging legs, coping with emergencies like the day the electric clippers passed out leaving one half of Goodwill unattractively hairy, and just enjoying the horses. These are never mere animals that have to be tended, that react to correct buttons being pressed when ridden. Mark's Favour, highly strung, typically feminine; Anne's superb, doughty Goodwill; the hot-tempered little chestnut, Flame Gun; her beloved, naughty Mardi Gras, that has given her more falls than any other horse; the good-looking Percy (Persian Holiday); like the dogs, Pleasure and Moriarty, that are Mark and Anne's boon companions, all the horses are well-loved personalities in their own right. The animals are an integrated part of their home life, sometimes the source of happy wrangling, as when Anne scandalizes Mark, a dedicated lover of thoroughbreds, by alluding to her well-bred Arthur of Troy as the stupidest horse she has ever known.

For the foreseeable future Mark is remaining in the army. One day he may revert to the farming life of his childhood, in which case Anne's feeling for the land and her inherited disregard of bad weather will stand her in good stead as a farmer's wife. Their hope is also to put to fuller use their extensive knowledge of horses.

Gatcombe Park lends itself to breeding, raising and schooling horses, to training and riding other people's eventers, to instructing or running a livery yard. This could be a commercial possibility and if, as must eventually occur, the Olympic Committee amend the rules on amateur status, then it will be possible to combine earning a living from horses with competitive aims and ambitions.

Continuing the royal duties that bring contact with people all over the world, the family they hope for eventually, a way of life that combines absorbing interest with income – that could well be the bright future the years have in store for Captain Mark Phillips and Her Royal Highness The Princess Anne, Mrs Mark Phillips, for Anne and Mark, who share their country life in the Cotswolds with their assortment of dogs and horses.

The Wedding Day

List of Plates

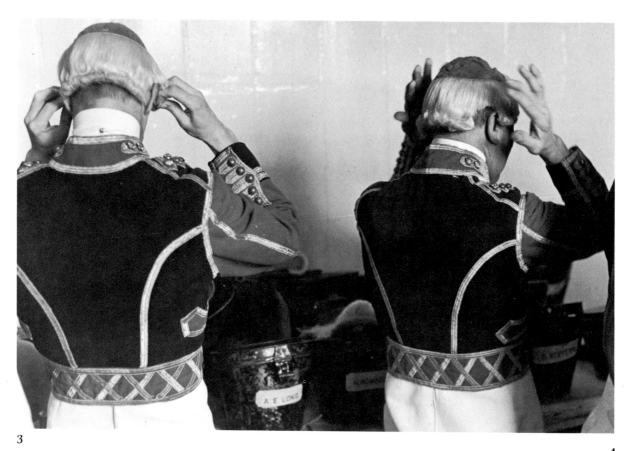

3

4

24

5

6

7

8

10

11

28

Royal Duties

List of Plates

14 ▷

16

19

20

21

23

24

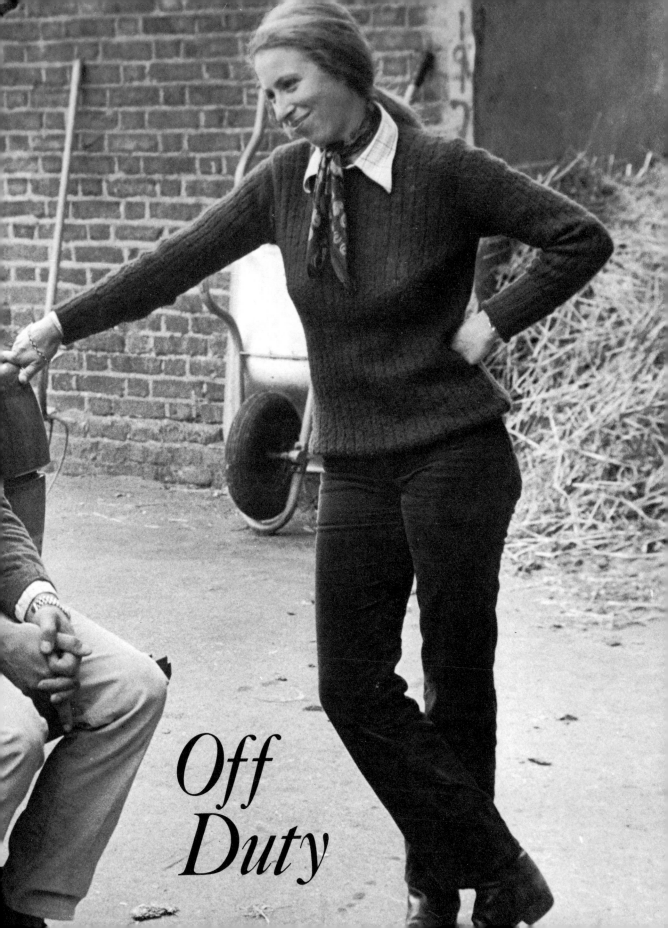

Off Duty

27

28

44

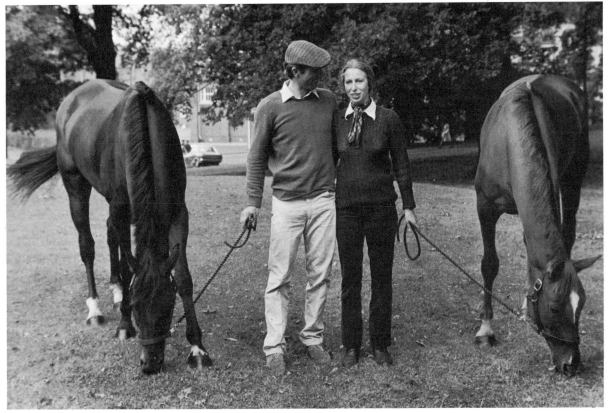

33

34

35

38 39 40 41

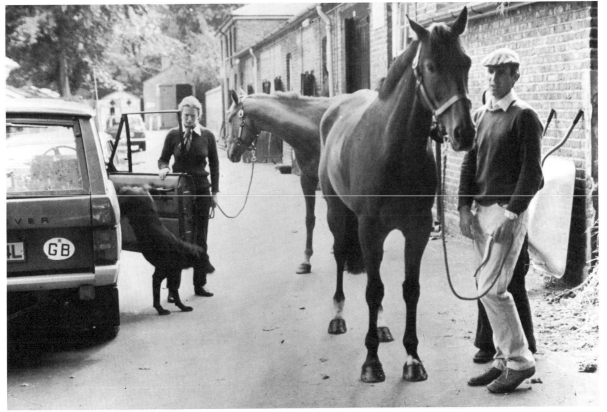

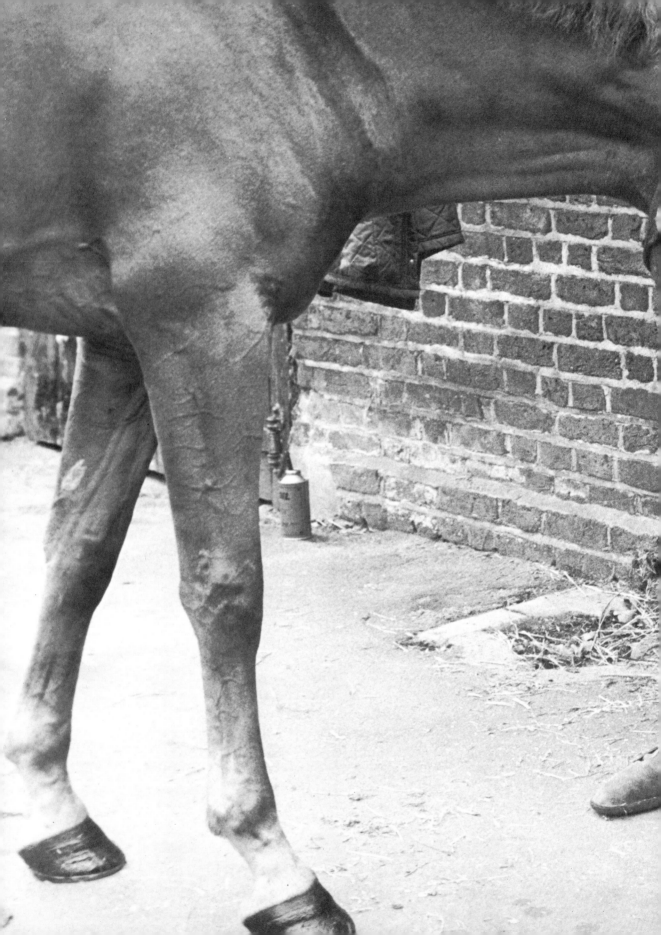

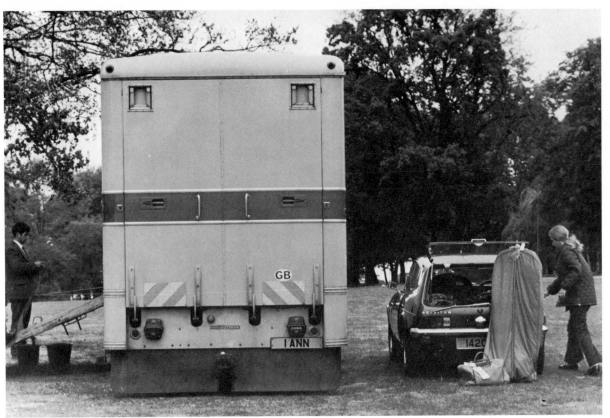

46

52

53

54

58

59

60

62

63

64

65

64

70

71

72

73

74

75

79

80

74

83

85

84

86

87

Anne
&
Mark

Previous page
In the grounds of Oak Grove House, 1975

This page
With Arthur of Troy (left), Flame Gun and their dog Moriarty

Opposite page
Top: With Mary Gordon-Watson, one of the leading British three-day event riders, Badminton, April 1972
Bottom left: Mark and Columbus, Badminton winners, 1973
Bottom right: Tidworth Horse Trials, autumn 1974

Above: Tidworth, summer 1974
Below: Burghley stables, 1974

Opposite page
At Windsor, 1974

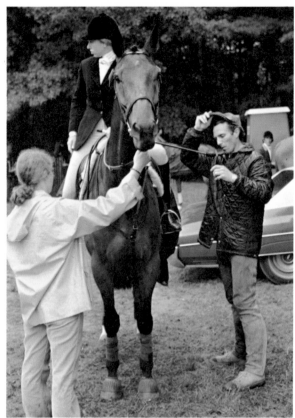

Above and left: A polishing for Anne's boots after rain in South Hamilton, U.S.A., summer 1975

Below: South Hamilton stables

Above : An afternoon ride outside Ledyard, Massachusetts, summer 1975   *Below :* Walking the course at Ledyard

Anne on Arthur of Troy, Goodwood, 1975

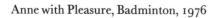
Anne with Pleasure, Badminton, 1976

Opposite page
Top: Mark on Favour, Badminton, 1975
Bottom: Anne with some of the young members of the
Riding for the Disabled Association, Liphook, 1975

Above and left: At a Great Somerford fête, Wilts., 1975
Below and opposite: Outside the stables at Sandhurst

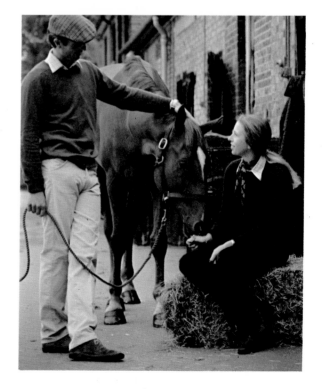

Above: On the balcony of Mansion House after receiving the Freedom of the City of London, 1976

Below: Arriving at the Guildhall before the ceremony

Anne on her way down the Mall after the Trooping the Colour ceremony, 1976

In the grounds of Oak Grove House

In Competition

93

94

95

96

99

100

105

109

110

113

114

112

115

120

121   122

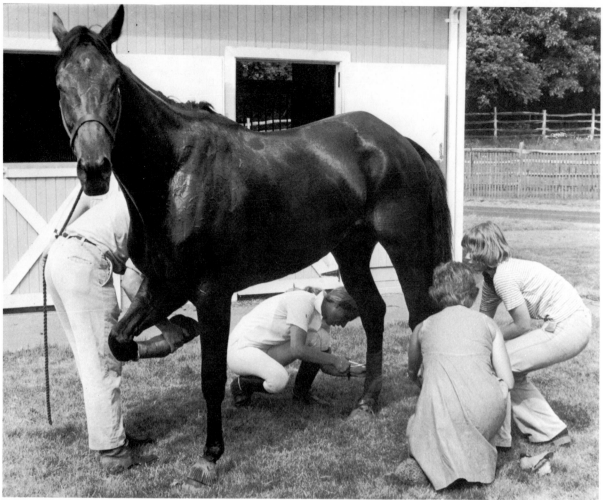

123

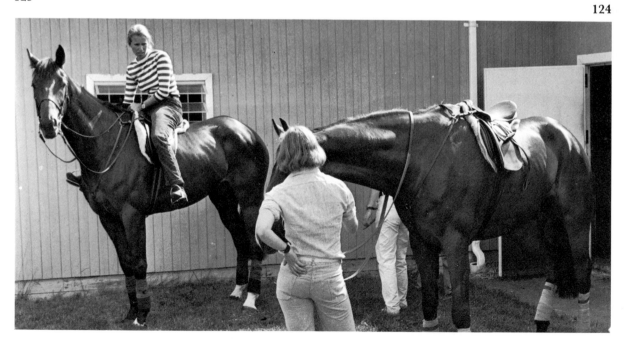

124

125

130 ▷

131 ▷

127

128

129

132

133

134

135

136

137

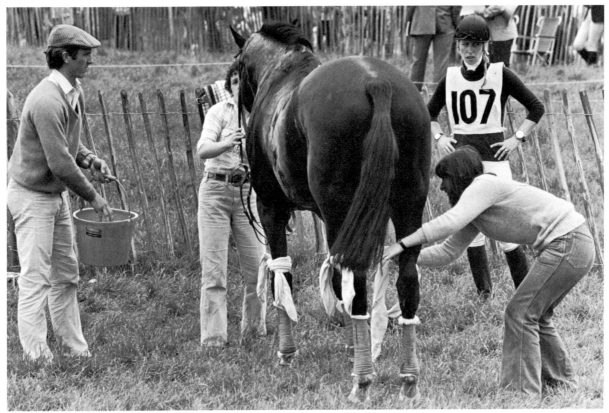

138

139

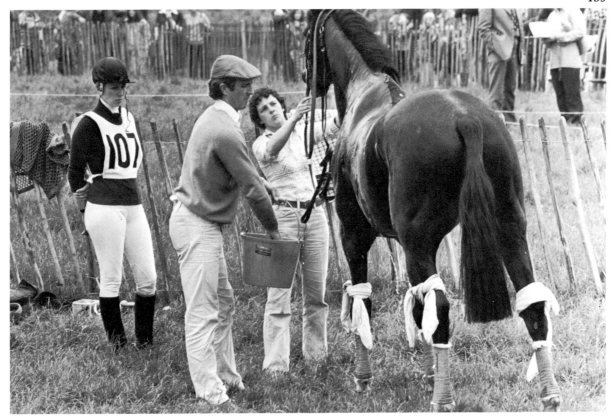

142

14[

144

145

146

154

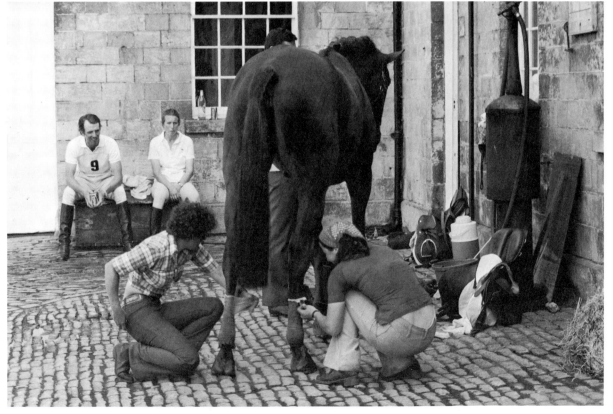

156

157

160

163

164

167

168

169

INDEX

Numbers in bold type refer to numbered plates, pp. 20-80, 97-143; numbers in italic type refer to pages on which unnumbered illustrations in colour or black and white appear.